Many people helped in the preparation of this book. Special thanks are due Kathy Mosolino, coach of the women's basketball team at Fordham College, and to these Fordham players who posed for photographs: Mary Gunning, Mary Hayes, Judy Puchalski, Karin Connelly, Mary Bilotti, Joanne Little, Ann Prunty, Liz McGovern, Kathy Sabo, Kim McAdams, and Anne Gregory. The author is also grateful to Gary Wagner, Wagner-International Photos, and Herb Field, Herb Field Studios.

Many experts name Carol Blazejowski as the finest women's basketball player of all time. She tallied a record 3,118 points during her career at Montclair (New Jersey) State, and her 52-point performance against Queens College in 1977 established the individual scoring record for Madison Square Garden.

BETTER BASKETBALL
for Girls

George Sullivan

DODD, MEAD & COMPANY · NEW YORK

Library of Congress Cataloging in Publication Data

Sullivan, George, 1927–
    Better basketball for girls.

    SUMMARY: Discusses the history, equipment, and techniques of women's basketball and includes a summary of the rules.
    1. Basketball for women—Juvenile literature. [1. Basketball for women] I. Title.
GV886.S9   796.32'38   78-7732
ISBN 0–396–07580–0

CONTENTS

Debbie Brock (right), 4-foot-11, 84 pounds, and a college star.

WOMEN AND BASKETBALL

A letter from a young woman appeared in *The Washington Post* in the early 1970s, accusing the paper of discrimination. "Girls' high school basketball scores are completely ignored in your paper," the letter declared, "while boys' high school basketball is given 500-word articles.

"There are numerous active, aggressive teams from all-girls' schools as well as public schools," the letter continued. "Girls' basketball is not a farce; it is an exciting spectator sport with a four-month season that is of interest to thousands of Washington-area students, including boys."

The lack of newspaper coverage at the time wasn't the only problem as far as girls' basketball was concerned. There were relatively few high school or college programs for girls or women. And when girls did get a chance to compete, they were seldom encouraged. Indeed, it was often said that women who participated in basketball—and other active sports—did so at the risk of their health and femininity.

Of course, that kind of thinking has gone the way of hoop skirts and crinolines.

Many things happened. The women's liberation movement stirred up interest in equality in sports. Women's physical education teachers began campaigning for athletic programs for girls. Congress passed legislation prohibiting discrimination in high school and college athletic programs.

As a result, hundreds of thousands of young women began taking part in competitive sports. Many of these women would have been spectators or cheerleaders a decade before.

For young women who want to play basketball, there is more opportunity to do so than ever before. There are organized teams in elementary schools, high schools, and colleges. Community gyms and many summer camps feature the sport. And don't overlook city playgrounds and suburban backyards.

Just as attitudes toward women's basketball have been changing, so has the game itself. In the past, women's basketball emphasized grace and shooting skill. It's somewhat different today. While the ability to put the ball in the basket is still essential, speed, strength, stamina, and aggressiveness are becoming more and more important.

There is also more of an emphasis on being tall. But this shouldn't discourage a prospective player who thinks she may lack in height. "If you're not particularly tall, you have to compensate in other ways," says Kathy Mosolino, basketball coach at Fordham College. "You have to excel on defense. You have to develop a good outside shot. You have to know how to dribble equally well with either hand and know how to feed the ball, be a play-maker."

Debbie Brock, 4-foot-11, 84 pounds, is the best evidence of this kind of thinking. From Forest Hill,

Mississippi, Debbie starred as a playmaking guard and ball-hawking defender for the Delta State Lady Statesmen, national college champions for three years in the late 1970s. "It's hard for other players to keep up with me," she was once quoted as saying, "because it's hard for them to find me." One opponent, frustrated by Debbie's speed and slipperiness, complained, "Next year we'll bring a fly-swatter."

Basketball was invented in 1891 by Dr. James A. Naismith, an instructor at the YMCA Training School in Springfield, Massachusetts. He was looking for an interesting game that could be played by his bored gym classes.

The game that Naismith thought up scarcely resembled basketball as it is played today. The ball was borrowed from soccer. The goals were peach baskets nailed to the lower rail of a gym balcony. There were nine players on a side. Only one basket was made in the first game.

There was one other difference. Naismith's game was all male.

But that changed within a matter of weeks. Teachers from nearby Buckingham Junior High School passed by the gym where Naismith's class was playing, watched a few games, and then formed the first girls' team.

The first women's college game was played at Smith College in Northhampton, Massachusetts, in

The Wellesley College team of 1895

1892. The first women's rulebook was published in 1899.

During the early 1900s, women played basketball in large numbers. "At Smith College, basketball leads all other athletic diversions by a large margin," said *Harper's Weekly* in February, 1902. "When a Smith girl becomes a good basketball player, she at once acquires athletic and social prominence in her college circles. To make the Sophomore or Freshman team is a distinction that she strives earnestly for."

Girls' games were often scheduled with boys' contests as double-headers in those days. But this

troubled many women. In 1923, Mrs. Herbert Hoover, the wife of the President, headed a national committee of women to investigate the practice of holding basketball double-headers. The committee was shocked to find that young women athletes were performing before audiences that included men. Mrs. Hoover and her committee declared the practice to be disgraceful and demanded that it be stopped. It was.

That was only the beginning. In the years that followed, state after state put an end to their athletic programs for young women. In states where athletic programs did continue, women were denied the

Smith College women of 1904. Notice the backboard; it's made of wire mesh.

Wellesley College women try an outdoor version of the game. This is 1904.

By early 1900s, women's basketball was well established in the West. This team represented the Southwestern State Normal School of Weatherford, Oklahoma. Coach is Ed Hickox, later first Executive Director of the National Basketball Hall of Fame.

opportunity to take part in any sport that was at all vigorous.

Women were regarded as fragile creatures. Sports, it was said, could destroy them.

Hygeia Magazine, in its issue of November, 1928, spoke about women athletes in these terms: "Girls are nervously more unstable than men and are consequently more affected in their way of distraction from their studies, in the loss of sleep before and after games and in general nervous injuries."

The magazine did not think well of basketball.

Uniforms had progressed to this stage by 1930s. These are Smith College players.

"On the physical side," the publication declared, "it is said that woman has a much smaller heart than man and that basketball involves a continual strain which a small heart is not well qualified to stand, often resulting in the girl's fainting or being unable to stand at the end of the half."

In time, of course, women began to challenge such beliefs and attitudes. Debate concerning the role of women grew heated during the 1960s. Women's liberation groups were formed to protest treatment women deemed to be unfair.

Laws were passed in the United States and Canada during the 1960s and early 1970s which were meant to ensure equal treatment for men and women. Nevertheless, as recently as 1973, *Sports Illustrated* could say: "There may be worse forms of prejudice in the United States, but there is no sharper example of discrimination today than that which operates against girls and women who take part in competitive sports, wish to take part, or might wish to if society did not scorn such endeavors."

A giant step forward was taken in 1972 when Congress passed amendments to the Civil Rights Act of 1964. Known as Title IX of the Federal Education Amendments of 1972, the law stated, "No person in the United States shall, on the basis of sex, be excluded from participation in, be denied the benefits of, or be subjected to discrimination under any education program or activity receiving

Federal financial assistance . . ."

Title IX meant that school classes and extracurricular activities had to be offered to all students. Girls could take auto maintenance and repair courses, if that's what they wanted. Boys could learn to cook in home economics classes.

Title IX also meant that school athletic programs had to include sports for girls. A period of enormous change followed. In 1970–71, a year before Title IX, only 294,000 girls (and 3,666,000 boys) competed in high school sports. By 1976–77, the number had increased to 1,645,000 girls (and 4,109,000 boys), a jump of 460 percent in six years.

In colleges, similar growth took place. The Association for Intercollegiate Athletics for Women (AIAW), the governing body of women's college sports, grew from 301 to 843 member schools in the same six-year period cited above. It is now the largest collegiate athletic association in the country, bigger than the National Collegiate Athletic Association (NCAA), the ruling body of men's college sports.

During the early 1970s, what was happening in women's basketball was often typified by a small, serene women's college near Paoli, Pennsylvania, a Philadelphia suburb. Immaculata was the name of the school. Cathy Rush was the name of the school's coach.

The team earned a 10-2 record in Rush's first year at Immaculata, but hardly anyone noticed.

Cathy Rush plots strategy with the Mighty Macs.

The school had no gym, so all the games had to be road games. Money was a problem. There were no leather basketballs, only rubber ones. Warm-up outfits didn't match. Sneakers sometimes didn't fit.

The next year Immaculata expanded its schedule, playing 25 games, again all on the road. By this time, Cathy Rush had molded the players into a well-disciplined, well-oiled unit that moved the ball with speed and precision and played a tenacious one-on-one defense.

The Mighty Macs, as they later were to be called, devoured the competition that season, ending with a 24-1 record. In the postseason tournament spon-

Signboard at Delta State campus salutes achievements of the Lady Statesmen.

sored by the Association for Intercollegiate Athletics for Women, Immaculata caught everybody by surprise, upsetting the Midwestern and Southern teams that had dominated women's basketball for years, and captured the championship.

That was in 1972. In 1973 and 1974, the phenomenal Macs repeated as AIAW champions. Things were different by that time. The results of Immaculata's games were being transmitted by the Associated Press to newspapers coast-to-coast. Never before had a national wire service paid any

attention to women's basketball.

Early in 1975, Immaculata became the first women's basketball team—along with Maryland—to appear on national television. A few weeks later, Immaculata faced Queens College of New York City at Madison Square Garden, becoming the first women's teams ever to play there.

The Macs finished second to Mississippi's Delta State in the AIAW tournament in 1975 and 1976, and ended up fourth in 1977. That same year Rush resigned as the Immaculata coach, saying she was "physically tired" and "basketball saturated."

Delta State won the AIAW title again in 1977. They thus equalled Immaculata's feat of winning three national championships in a row. But by the end of the decade both Delta State and Immaculata had been shouldered out of the spotlight by the more traditional collegiate sports powers, by such teams as Louisiana State, North Carolina State, Tennessee, UCLA, and Maryland.

Women's basketball today is a far cry from what it was in the early 1970s. In terms of the number of participants and their skill, spectator interest, and the attitude of the press and television, the sport has been transformed.

"I knew we'd win acceptance one day," Cathy Rush could say in 1977. "But I didn't expect anything like this. It's all very gratifying and maybe a little astounding, how far we've progressed in just this decade."

ridges that run crosswise. You may also see basketball shoes with soles made of small upraised circles.

Whether it's ridged soles or not, you need good support for your feet. Leather or suede sneakers provide the most support.

Sneakers of these materials will conform to the exact shape of your foot; canvas and nylon sneakers won't. However, canvas and nylon are fabrics that "breathe" better and dry faster.

Getting the right fit is vital, of course. When you begin playing basketball seriously, you should wear two pairs of socks to protect your feet. So when you go shopping for sneakers, be sure to wear two pairs of socks so you'll get the right fit. Even then, allow about a quarter of an inch leeway in the toe, because after running strenuously on the court for a while, your feet swell.

Ridged soles, right, are typical for basketball sneakers.

Below: Most players prefer low-cuts.

Up until very recent times, women athletes had to buy men's sneakers. The rule of thumb was that a woman bought men's shoes that were one-and-one-half or two sizes smaller than her own. Thus, a woman with a size 7 foot bought men's shoes size 5½ or 5. This situation is changing. Most manufacturers now acknowledge that women's feet are generally narrower and shorter than men's and are beginning to sell sneakers in women's sizes. Women's sneakers have such nicknames as Dove, Wellesley, and Lady Dragon.

If you're going to be playing most of your basketball on outdoor courts, on concrete or asphalt, that is, you'll want sneakers that are going to wear longer. Buy sneakers with polyurethane soles. They are more durable than rubber soles and they cost less.

Since sneakers are available in so many varieties, it's not surprising that different methods of keeping them clean have evolved. Soap and water and a stiff-bristle brush are what to use on canvas or nylon sneakers. Use a suede cleaner on leather sneakers.

If you become attached to a pair of sneakers and don't feel like throwing them away after the soles have worn down, you can probably get them resoled. More and more shoe repair shops are offering this service. Specialists in the field advertise in the pages of the leading tennis magazines.

Normally, you should get about a season of use from a pair of sneakers. With a retread job, you can double their lifetime.

HOW TO CATCH THE BALL

Most players think they know how to catch the ball, and, indeed, they are able to handle most passes that come to them without trouble. But there are a couple of "secrets" about catching the ball that you should know. Once you know them, you should never miss a pass.

Suppose the ball comes to you above your waist. Face your palms toward the ball, the thumbs almost touching.

What you should not do is attempt to catch the ball by grasping it at each side. If you don't get your thumbs behind the ball, it can easily slip through your fingers.

When the ball arrives below waist level, point the fingers toward the floor and again face the palms toward the ball. This time your little fingers should be almost touching.

Follow the ball all the way to your hands with your eyes. This sounds obvious, but some players develop a habit of taking their eyes off the ball—to

When you're receiving a pass, first face your palms toward the ball. Squeeze the ball when it comes; move it to one side.

Anytime you're going to receive the ball, give your teammate a target at which to shoot. Extend your hands and arms, indicating where you want to receive the ball, high or low or to the left or right.

If you're taller than average, use your height; raise the ball out of danger after you make the catch.

look at the basket or for someone to pass to—at the last moment. The result is a fumble.

Squeeze the ball when it arrives, tightening your grip. Draw it close to your body.

If you're taller than average, don't make the mistake of holding the ball at waist level after you receive it. Use your height, that is, raise the ball at the level of your shoulders or even higher.

No matter how tall you happen to be, never hold the ball in front of your body. An opposing player can easily whack it away. Instead, hold it to one side, protecting it with your body. If an opponent comes at you from that side, shift the ball to the other side.

19

YOUR STANCE

Before you begin to sharpen your skills in shooting, passing, and dribbling, you should be certain that you know the basic "ready" position common to basketball. From this stance, you're able to move quickly forward or back or to either side.

To assume a correct stance, spread your feet wide apart, at least as wide apart as the width of your shoulders. Bend in the knees and lean backward slightly, lowering your seat. Turn your knees outward, the way a catcher does in baseball.

Straighten your upper body. Keep your chin up. Keep your hands in front of you, as if you were expecting to catch a pass.

The stance position is awkward for some women. What bothers them is standing with the legs wide apart and the knees turned out.

Practice at home in front of a mirror until the stance feels comfortable to you. Since it is the basic position from which all court movement begins, it's important to get it perfectly right.

Your stance should enable you to move quickly forward or back or to either side.

HOW TO DRIBBLE

To dribble, according to the dictionary, is to move a ball by repeated bounces. It's not a difficult skill to learn.

When you dribble, bend from the waist and bend in the knees. This helps you to keep the ball low. Keep your back straight, your head erect.

Don't permit the ball to bounce any higher than waist level. The higher it bounces, the greater the chance that it can be knocked away or stolen away by an opponent.

As you dribble, protect the ball by positioning your body between the ball and the player who is guarding you. You can also shield the ball by using your free arm in protective fashion.

During practice sessions, try dribbling with one hand and then the other. In time, you should become able to dribble with equal skill with either hand.

When you dribble, bend low; keep the ball low.

You should be able to dribble as well with your left hand as you do with your right.

When you are able to dribble with either hand, you'll be able to perform crossover moves. Suppose you're dribbling with your right hand and an opponent blocks your way. You pull the ball back toward your feet, bounce it from right to left across your body and pick it up with your left hand. You then pivot and head off toward the left, dribbling with the left hand.

The ability to dribble with either hand also enables you to execute a reverse pivot. You're dribbling forward; as an opponent moves to defend, you spin your body away from the player, turning a full 180 degrees. You then switch dribbling hands and dart off in the other direction. It all happens in the blink of an eye.

Most young players have no difficulty in learning how to dribble. But learning *when* to dribble is another matter.

When you receive the ball, you should never dribble immediately. Dribbling is the slowest method there is of advancing the ball. It gives the defense time to organize and set up its coverage.

As soon as you get your hands on the ball, pivot to face the basket and then look for an open player to pass to. Or if you have an opportunity to score, then by all means shoot. It's usually only when you can't pass and can't shoot that you should dribble.

HOW TO PASS

Teamwork is what makes a winner. And passing is the essence of good teamwork.

Each one of several different types of passes is explained in the pages that follow. No matter which type you happen to be using, always aim for a specific target. Your teammate, by extending her hands and arms, is likely to tell you where she wants the ball. But if she fails to do this, it's up to you to decide where and how to pass the ball.

If there's a defensive player at your teammate's right, then pass the ball to her left. If your teammate is tall, then don't target the ball at her knees.

If she's near to you, don't throw the ball so hard that she won't be able to control it. If she's far down the court, don't lob the ball; it's likely to be intercepted.

There are four basic types of passes: the chest pass, the bounce pass, the overhead pass, and the baseball pass. Certain characteristics apply to each of them. Always step in the direction of the pass, getting the momentum of your body into the throw. Always follow through, straightening your arms, or arm, as you release.

THE CHEST PASS—The chest pass is the safest and most widely used of all passes. As you grip the ball to deliver a chest pass, holding it close to your

In delivering a chest pass, step toward your target. Put wrist snap into the throw; remember to follow through.

For the chest pass, position hands like this.

chest, the thumbs should be behind the ball, almost touching.

Step toward your target, pushing the ball away from your body, straightening your arms and snapping the wrists forward. It's this wrist snap that gives zip to the pass.

After you've delivered the ball, check your fingers. They should be pointing directly at the person who's received the pass.

THE BOUNCE PASS—The bounce pass, in which you rebound the ball off the floor to a teammate, is delivered with the same motion you use for the chest pass. But instead of the fingers pointing to the receiver as you follow through, they should point to the spot on the floor where the ball bounced.

When throwing a bounce pass, start it at about waist level. This enables you to get your upper body into the throw. A bounce pass thrown from shoulder or chest level is likely to lack in both speed and accuracy.

Time the pass so that it bounces well beyond the midpoint of the distance the ball is to travel. When the bounce is closer to you than it is to the receiver, the ball is more likely to be intercepted. When the ball rebounds close to the receiver, the narrow angle of the bounce enables her to catch the ball with greater ease.

The bounce pass is usually the pass to use when you're trying to get the ball to a teammate who is racing for the basket. Since the bounce slows the

The overhead pass requires a step and wrist snap, too.

ball's speed, it's easier for her to handle. In addition, since the ball is bouncing up toward the receiver, she can treat it as a dribble if she wants, bouncing it once or twice before shooting.

The bounce pass can be troublesome for the defense. Tall defensive centers and forwards, who are guarding the area where the bounce pass is usually used, have difficulty reaching down in attempting to retrieve low passes.

But keep in mind that the bounce pass is not perfect. Since its speed is relatively slow, it gives the defense an extra split second or two to react, to intercept or knock the ball away. Use it with caution.

THE OVERHEAD PASS—The overhead pass is another two-handed pass which is thrown with the thumbs behind the ball, and delivered with the same arm-straightening, wrist-snapping motion as the chest pass.

As you get set to throw, position the ball above your head. Your arms should be almost straight. Don't make the mistake of positioning the ball *behind* your head. Do so, and you're not likely to be accurate with the throw. A good follow-through is important.

The overhead pass, since it has good velocity, is often used as an outlet pass, the pass that triggers a fast break after a rebound or a steal.

THE BASEBALL PASS—The baseball pass is so named because it is said to resemble the throw a catcher makes to second base. It's an overhand

With the baseball pass, get your hand behind the ball. Again, stride forward as you deliver.

throw, delivered from close to the right ear.

Get your fingers behind the ball as you prepare to throw. Use your other hand, the left hand, to help keep the ball balanced. Stride forward as you deliver, getting your upper body behind the throw.

While it doesn't have the velocity or accuracy of a chest pass, the baseball pass is acceptable when you have to throw the ball a long way.

There are many other types of passes. There's the dribble pass in which a player who is dribbling suddenly cuts away from the ball and lets a teammate retrieve it. There's the hook pass, delivered with a mighty sweep of the arm. There is a short shovel pass and the long lob. There's the flashy behind-the-back pass. But don't attempt any of these until you're more experienced. Concentrate on the four basic passes. They're the easiest to learn and there is much less risk involved in their use.

No matter what type of pass you're throwing, try not to "telegraph" it, that is, don't tip off where you're planning to throw the ball by staring at your receiver. Instead, try to be deceptive. If you're throwing an overhead pass, fake throwing it first, bringing your arms forward but not releasing the ball. You may be able to get a defensive player to react, in which case she's likely to be out of position when you actually throw the ball.

Experienced players can sometimes fake a two-hand chest pass in one direction, then throw a one-hand pass in another direction. Try this in a practice session. You can use your head or your shoulders to feint the direction of a pass.

To become a good passer, you must practice. You can practice by yourself, simply throwing the ball against a wall and letting it rebound. Throw five chest passes, then five bounce passes, and so on. Be sure your form is perfect each time you throw.

It's better to practice with a teammate, of course. One good drill is to throw the ball back and forth, seeing how many passes the two of you can complete in a specified period of time without missing.

Another passing drill involves using two balls. As you throw, so does your teammate. This exercise not only sharpens your passing ability, but can also serve to improve your reaction time.

HOW TO SHOOT

"Male basketball players may be taller, quicker, and stronger, but they're not necessarily better shooters," says Mary Lou Johns, women's basketball coach at Memphis State University. "When it comes to shooting the basketball, the good female basketball player can shoot right along with the best of the men since coordination is the main ingredient in shooting the ball."

While each player develops her own shooting style, there are certain fundamentals that are important. You should be facing the basket when you're getting set to shoot, and you must have the ball under control. You should follow through with your hands and arms in every shot. A good follow-through helps to make you accurate.

It's also vital to aim *into* the basket, not merely throw in the general direction of the rim. Beginners are usually instructed to aim over the rim on all shots except lay-ups, in which case the ball is to be rebounded off the backboard.

There are three basic shots: the push shot, the jump shot, and the lay-up. You should become equally skilled in the use of each. The hook shot is also described in this section. But it's not a shot the beginner has to know; it's for the advanced player.

THE PUSH SHOT—The push shot is the best shot to learn first because it includes many of the techniques you have to know in executing most other

In the push shot, the hand should support the ball like this.

27

Sink in the knees as you get set; cock your right arm and wrist. Straighten your legs as you release. Follow through.

shots. Work to develop a good push shot and you should have no trouble with the jump shot or foul shooting.

In trying a push shot, stand with your feet about shoulder-width apart, your toes pointing toward the basket. If you're a right-handed shooter, your right foot should be slightly ahead of your left. Your knees should be slightly bent. Your weight should be on the balls of your feet. Overall, you should be well-balanced and comfortable.

Hold the ball high, just to the right of your right eye, supporting it with your fingers from behind. Your forearm should be at right angles to the floor. the elbow pointing in the direction of the basket.

Use your left hand to help get and keep the ball balanced.

Take careful aim, focusing your eyes on an imaginary spot just over the rim of the basket.

As you begin the shot, sink a bit more in the knees. Keep the ball in the same position.

Use your whole body in delivering the ball, straightening your legs, extending your arm straight up in the air, and snapping your wrist forward. The ball should roll off your fingers with plenty of backspin, sailing in a high arc.

The push shot is a very reliable shot. You'll want to use it anytime you're not being closely guarded.

THE JUMP SHOT—Up until ten or fifteen years ago, the jump shot was almost unknown. Coaches wanted their players to shoot only when they had both feet on the floor. That kind of thinking has gone the way of six-girl teams.

Today, the jump shot is used more frequently than any other. You can toss one up off a dribble, off a rebound, or from a set position. It's always a problem for the defender.

The jump shot is a push shot with a properly timed jump. The ball must be released at the peak of the jump. There is a split second that you are suspended in the air—you're as high as you're going to go; you haven't yet started to come down—and that's when the ball should be pushed away. Shooting before or after you reach the peak of the jump hurts your accuracy.

It's almost impossible to stop a well-executed jump shot.

Get set; take careful aim; release the ball at the peak of the jump.

As you flex your knees and get set to jump, raise the ball to at least shoulder level. Your right hand supports the ball; cock your right wrist. Jump as high as you can. This enables you to get a clear view of the basket rim and makes the defensive player's job more difficult. Raise the ball above your head and flip it away.

Learn to combine fake movements with your jump shot. Feint with your hands or head before you go up. If you execute a good fake and the player defending you leaps up to block the "shot," you can go up for a clear shot as she is coming down. This is likely to happen several times during the average game.

To be successful with the jump shot, you should be able to visualize what it entails, that is, you should know exactly what you look like at the highest point of the jump. The next time you attend a basketball game or watch one on television, study the players as they execute jump shots. Try to fix in your mind's eye how their arms and legs are positioned as they release the ball. This mental image will help you in attaining the proper body position on jump shots of your own.

THE LAY-UP—A one-hand, banked shot made at the end of a drive, the lay-up is the simplest of all shots because you're so close to the basket when the ball is released. You simply "lay" the ball against the backboard and it rebounds into the basket.

In both the push and jump shots, the wrist flips forward to give power and direction to the shot.

In executing a lay-up from the right side of the basket, go up on your left foot. It's a hop step. Push the ball against the backboard, letting it drop into the basket.

If you're a right-handed shooter, you go into the basket from the right side, pushing off with your left foot, lifting the right leg as high as possible. Push the ball toward the backboard and let it drop through the hoop.

Suppose you're a beginner and want to learn how to shoot a lay-up. Try this drill: Stand near the backboard just to the right of the basket. Hold the ball in both hands. Now, shoot; push the ball with your right hand toward the backboard, aiming at a spot above and to the right of the basket. At the same time your right hand goes up, push from the left foot, lifting the right leg. This leg action will make it easy for you to get the ball high up on the backboard.

As you continue the drill, put more and more emphasis on the leg action. Take off on your left foot and come down on it again as you push the ball away. It's a hop step.

Once you've become skilled in making lay-ups from this standing-still position, try a two-step lay-up—step right, then left. On the step with your left foot, leap and shoot. Keep practicing this drill until you can perform it at top speed. Then back up farther, and try adding a dribble or two to the exercise. You always end up in the same fashion, going in from the right side, shooting with the right hand, pushing off from the left foot.

If you're a right-hander, shooting lay-ups from the left side is likely to feel awkward to you. Beginners shouldn't worry about this. Later, you'll want to learn how to shoot lay-ups from the left side

using your left hand. But for now concentrate on the right side and using your right hand.

Shooting lay-ups during a game is much different from shooting them during a practice drill. Statistics show that high school players are successful on about 85 percent of their lay-up attempts. They miss because of the actions of the defensive players.

You must concentrate; you can't let yourself be distracted by the defense.

When you drive in for a lay-up, a defender is likely to be shouting at you or waving her hands in your face—or both. But you can't allow yourself to be distracted. You must keep your attention focused on your target; you can't look away, not even for a part of a second.

THE HOOK SHOT—Like the jump shot, the hook shot is almost impossible to defend against when it's executed correctly. The reason it's not used more frequently is because it's not as easy as the jump shot. It's not a shot beginners should attempt.

Centers and forwards use the hook the most. It's sometimes useful in drawing fouls, and faking a hook shot is one way to pave the way for a push shot or a jumper.

You deliver the hook shot with one hand over your head while you are sideways to the basket. Once you're in position, hold the ball with both hands and stride forward on your left foot. Your right hand begins its upward sweep; your wrist is cocked.

Raise yourself up onto the toes of your left foot. Release the ball as the right hand reaches the highest point of its arc.

The hook shot requires more practice than any other shot. But even those players who become skilled in its use don't use it on any more than 3 or 4 percent of their shots.

The hook shot is delivered with a long upward sweep of the right arm.

FOUL SHOOTING

Foul shooting is both easy and difficult. It's easy because there's no defensive player guarding you as you shoot. But it's difficult because you have a great deal to think about and plenty of time in which to do that thinking. This can hurt your performance—if you let it.

Players today prefer the one-hand push shot for free throws. It's described and pictured in the previous section.

Take your time getting set. The rulebook says that after you've been awarded the ball by the referee, you have ten seconds in which to prepare yourself. Set the ball seams so they're at right angles to your fingers. Check your feet; they must be in back of the free-throw line. It's a good idea to position yourself and your feet exactly the same way each time you take a foul shot.

Relax. Take a deep breath. Bounce the ball a few times, if you feel it helps. Concentrate. Keep your eyes on your target. As you raise the ball and fire, imagine the path the ball is going to take to the hoop.

Occasionally you will see a player who prefers to use a two-hand underhand shot instead of a one-hand push shot in shooting fouls. To execute this shot, spread your legs, sink deep in the knees, and lower the ball between your knees to about knee level. You then raise the ball in one rhythmic

Relax; take your time getting set.

sweep, releasing it at about eye level as you come to a standing position.

One failing of the two-hand underhand shot is that it can be used only for foul shooting. It has no other offensive value. That's why coaches don't recommend its use. They would rather see their players become skilled with the one-hand push shot and concentrate on it during practice sessions.

If you play for a high school team, your coach won't be unhappy if you are successful on seven out of every ten of your free-throw attempts. Keeping track of your free-throw percentage can help you to improve. For each game, and for each practice session and pick-up game, as well, record how many free throws you attempt and how many you make. Doing so will help to make you more serious-minded whenever you step to the foul line.

Some coaches instruct their players to take fifty shots when practicing free throws. If you follow this plan, or one that's similar, take your time on each shot. Check your grip and your feet. Relax; take a deep breath. Push the ball away; follow through. Follow exactly the same procedure on every throw.

Most players use a one-hand push shot from the free-throw line.

35

JUMP BALLS

In high school competition, each quarter begins with a jump ball, one player opposing the other within the center circle. Usually the two players are the teams' centers.

Jump balls are also called when two opposing players contact the ball simultaneously, causing it to go out of bounds. Tie-ball and held-ball situations call for jump balls, too. A tie ball occurs when two opposing players struggle for the ball, and neither is able to get possession. A held ball is called when a player holds the ball for more than five seconds while being closely guarded.

As these rules imply, a jump ball can be called at anytime during a game, and any member of a team can be called upon to do the jumping.

Let's say that you're involved in a jump-ball call, and you're lining up in the restraining circle opposite your opponent. You must remain within that half of the circle that is closest to the basket you're defending. In other words, you're facing the opposition basket.

One foot must be near the circle's center line. Your teammates take up positions outside the circle, and they must hold to those positions until the ball is tapped.

An official tosses the ball up between you and your opponent. How high does she toss it? The rules say "to a height that is greater than both opponents

Get comfortable as you prepare to jump; crouch down.

can reach." If the ball should fall to the floor without either of you tapping it, the play must be repeated.

Get comfortable as you prepare to jump. Spread your feet until they're about shoulder-width apart. Concentrate on the official's hands as she gets set to toss.

When the official starts the ball upward, take a short step with your front foot toward your op-

As you leap, keep your eye on the ball.

ponent, raise your forearms, and crouch down. Now your body is coiled, ready to leap.

Keep your eyes on the ball as it goes up. Time your jump so that you can tap it at the highest point

Tap the ball at the highest point of your leap.

of your leap. Don't try to slap the ball with your open hand. Instead, use the tips of the three middle

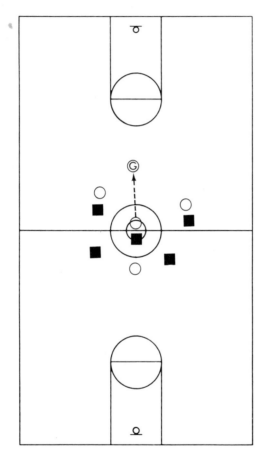

This is a defensive tap, with the ball going back to a playmaking guard (G).

fingers on the bottom of the ball, tapping the ball forward or back, to the right or left.

When you come down, land with your weight on the balls of your feet, ready to move in any direction.

Unless you're considerably taller than 6 feet, there are going to be jump-ball situations in which you are overmatched. One piece of strategy that you can use against a much taller opponent is to jump early, as the ball is on its way up, but withhold your tap. When your opponent sees you leap, she may go up, too, and tap the ball before it has reached its highest point. This is a violation of the rules, and your team will be awarded the ball out of bounds.

Another tactic you can try against a taller opponent is to strike her hand or forearm with your hand as you follow through. If you're lucky, this can cause her tap to go amiss, and the ball may end up in the hands of one of your teammates.

Precisely where you try to tap the ball on jump-ball plays depends on your team's strategy, that is, how your coach has instructed your teammates to align themselves. Teams sometimes line up with two tall players (usually two forwards) on the same side of the circle as the jumper. A third player is stationed between these two players, and a step or two closer to the basket. The fourth player is positioned on the circle's edge opposite the jumper.

This is essentially a defensive formation. It's used

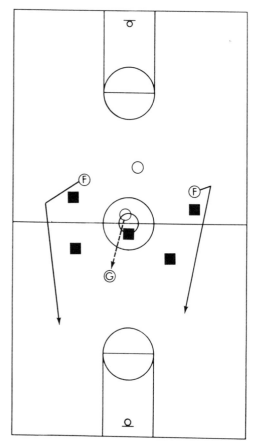

This is the tap a team on the attack might use, with the forwards (F) cutting toward the basket in anticipation of a pass from the guard.

when a team must have possession; for example, in the game's closing minute by a team that is leading by a point or two. The strategy is to tap the ball to the deep girl. Each of the forwards screens out an opposition player so that the deep girl will not be interfered with as she moves to receive the ball.

This alignment can easily be converted to an offensive play. Just as the ball is about to be tapped, one of the forwards breaks around the circle and cuts toward the opposition basket. The tap goes to the other guard, and she passes to the forward who is breaking downcourt.

If you're seeking to become a better jumper, skipping rope is a good exercise. You can also try a drill in which you stand beneath the basket rim and jump up and touch the net—or try to.

GETTING FREE

How much shooting and passing you're able to do during a game depends to some extent on how successful you are in outwitting and outmaneuvering the defender you face. In the early stages of the game, learn as much as you can about her style of play, and then adjust *your* game accordingly.

How closely does she play you? If she plays you loose, you're going to have opportunities to shoot and pass. If she plays you tight, you're going to have to try driving by her, using a low dribble.

There are several standard methods of attempting to outwit an opponent. Unless you know how to execute these feints, you will seldom have a clear driving lane or enough room to shoot or pass.

The step fake is one such feint. You thrust your foot and leg forward toward your opponent. Lean forward, too. Make it look convincing. Watch her reaction. If she retreats, pull your foot back and shoot.

Suppose she doesn't take the fake, but simply stays in her original position. Then use a crossover step to drive by her. Let's say you've stepped forward with the right foot and leg. To cross over, move the foot to your left, crossing it in front of the left foot, and speed off in that direction, dribbling with your left hand. Your body, between the defender and the ball, protects the ball from being stolen. Keeping your body low and controlling the dribble is important, too.

Notice how she positions her hands when she guards you. Check to see how her weight is balanced. Does she try to steal the ball from you? If she does, you might invite a steal attempt by dribbling close to her. When she flicks her hand out, suddenly change direction or pass.

41

OTHER OFFENSIVE SKILLS

Knowing how to shoot is essential and being a good passer is vital, too, but there are several other skills that you must develop in order to become a complete player.

Whenever a teammate has the ball, it's your job to get free for a pass.

Look at it this way: In a high school game, which is 32 minutes in length, your team will have the ball about half the time, or about 16 minutes. Since the team is made up of five players, that means that you will handle the ball about one-fifth of the time—between three and four minutes. For the other 12 or 13 minutes, you'll be doing other things, such as cutting toward the basket, setting up screens for your teammates, or rebounding.

Whenever your team is on the attack and another player has the ball, your number one job is to get free for a possible pass. Getting free requires the ability to react to the moves of the player who is guarding you. Great speed isn't a requirement, but quickness is. You have to be able to start fast, to dart one way and the other like a frightened hare, using pivots, feints, turns, and quick changes in speed and direction as you move.

Try different kinds of feints early in the game to determine whether the player guarding you can be beaten with any of them. The step fake is standard. Fake a step toward the defender. When she reacts by stepping back to block your path, you're open; turn toward your teammate with the ball and reach out to receive a pass.

A variation of this move is to execute a reverse spin after the fake step. Again you're being guarded by a defender who is positioned between you and the basket. Suddenly step toward her with your left foot, then, pivoting toward your right on your right foot, you turn your back to the defender. Now you're open for a pass.

You can also use a backdoor route in getting open. Imagine your teammate has the ball near the top of the key. (The key is the entire free-throw

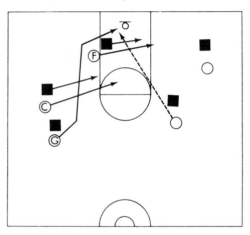

area, including the free-throw lane and circle.) You, playing guard (G), are positioned on the left side not far from the free-throw lane. A defender is between you and the basket.

Cut suddenly behind your defender and toward the baseline, and then go for the basket. The forward (F) and center (C) clear your path by decoying enemy players. You should get a pass right under the basket. An easy lay-up is the result.

Keep alert for cutting opportunities. You can sometimes cut successfully after passing. Your defender, upon seeing you give up possession of the ball, may relax for a moment. Or it may be that she's pulled herself out of position by attempting to block the pass. That's your chance.

Sometimes when you're planning to cut, you can use a teammate to screen the player who's defending you. As you dash by, cut closely to your teammate so she'll block the path of your defender. If the opposition players don't call a switch, you'll be clear for a pass.

Player on the right screens off the defender, allowing player on left to shoot.

SCREENS AND PICKS

Many times during a game you'll have the assistance of a teammate when you're trying to get free of a player who is covering you.

Say you have the ball and you're driving toward the basket. A teammate, her back to the basket, takes a step or two toward you and plants her feet firmly, effectively "screening out" your defender. You're then free to shoot or pass.

Of course, you may not have to stop and shoot. If your path is clear, you can drive to the basket and lay the ball up. In this case, the screen becomes a pick. Your teammate has "picked off" the player covering you.

One mistaken notion about screens is that the player setting the screen is the one responsible for

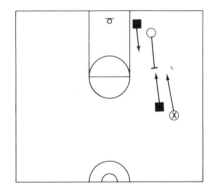

A simple screen play, with player advancing from the baseline to set screen for the ball handler (X).

its success. Not at all. The player with the ball must drive properly in order to make the play work. She has to drive so closely to her teammate's shoulder that she almost touches her; otherwise, the defending player isn't likely to be screened or picked.

A fake can be helpful in making a screen play successful. You, as the ball handler, should try first faking to the left before driving toward a screen being set on the right.

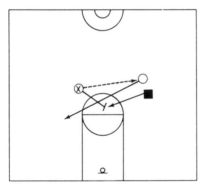

In this screen play, ball handler (X) first passes to a teammate, then darts to the top of the key to screen defender.

Sometimes a defensive player is able to anticipate what's happening. As she becomes aware that a screen is being set, she circles behind the player setting up the screen and intercepts you, the ball handler, on the other side.

A change in strategy is in order when you see this happening. Stop in front of your teammate who is setting the screen and shoot over her. Caught out of position, the defensive player won't have a chance to get close enough to block your shot.

Defensive players also try to foil screen plays by switching. Suppose you're the ball handler again, and you're driving toward the basket, using a teammate's screen to cut off the defender. The defensive player who is guarding your teammate sees what's happening and shouts out, "Switch!" She then drops off your teammate and darts over to block your path to the basket. The opponent who was guarding you now covers your teammate.

Now is the time for some counterstrategy. Your teammate should pivot toward you, putting her back to the defender. You toss her the ball; she has a clear shot.

Here, ball handler (X) is able to drive to the basket, thanks to teammate's pick.

REBOUNDING

While being tall is a big advantage when you're leaping up to try to get a missed shot off the backboard, it isn't necessarily the most important quality that you can have. Aggressiveness counts for a great deal. You have to be determined when you go up for the ball, exploding into the air. You have to be bold.

You also have to accept the fact that there's going to be body contact, since there are other people who are going to be after the ball. Be prepared to get thumped once in a while.

As you get set to jump up for the ball, spread your feet wide apart. Bend in the knees. Your weight should be on the balls of your feet. Time yourself so that you reach the ball at the very peak of your jump and with your arms fully extended.

Squeeze the ball as you grasp it. Then, while you're still in the air, bring the ball down to the level of your chin, keeping your elbows out to protect it. What you must avoid doing is landing with the ball held over your head. It can easily be knocked away or even stolen by an opponent.

As you're coming down, make a half turn away from the basket. Land on the balls of your feet, your legs well spread. The ball should still be at chin level. Your elbows should still be pointing outward protectively.

Coaches classify rebounds as being either defensive or offensive in nature. A defensive rebound

Get both hands on the ball; squeeze tightly.

occurs after a missed shot by the opposition; in other words, it's a shot toward the goal you're defending. An offensive rebound occurs after your team misses a shot.

Defensive rebounds are easier to get, because when you're defending, your team is likely to be closer to the basket than the opposition. It's important to block out an opponent in order to maintain this advantage, a strategy that is known as "boxing out."

As the shot is being taken, turn your back to your opponent, and position yourself between her and the basket. Then back into her. "Sit on her thighs," is what one coach tells her players. Keep your elbows out. You're trying to make it impossible for her to get to the basket, to the rebound.

The strategy of boxing out has one drawback. Should any member of the defensive team fail to do her job and not box out her opponent, the opposition player who slips through has a good chance of getting the rebound.

When you box out, be careful not to contact your opponent with your hands or arms. A foul can be the result. Instead, your hands should be up, your elbows out, as you get set to jump. When the ball comes down, go and get it, leaving the opponent behind.

Once you have the ball in your possession near the defensive boards, you must make the pass that triggers the fast break. It's called an "outlet pass." It has to be done quickly, before the defense has a chance to react. Never lob the ball; pass crisply.

Pass to someone on the same side of the court as you are. It's dangerous to pass the ball from one side of the court to the other in front of the basket you're defending. An interception is almost surely to result in two points for the opposition.

Offensive rebounding is rougher. You're farther away from the basket and an opponent is likely to try to box you out. Getting to the ball can be a struggle.

Try to keep a good distance between yourself and the opponent who is attempting to cover you. The more room you have, the better you can maneuver.

Watch your opponent carefully. Whenever she takes her eyes off you, you have a chance to drive in. Sometimes you'll be able to elude an opponent by faking a cut in one direction and actually cutting in the direction opposite.

One advantage that you have when your team is on the attack is that you know when your teammate is going to shoot. You should be able to use this

This is boxing out—blocking an opponent from the rebound.

A tap-in; try to use two hands.

knowledge to gain a half step on your opponent in scrambling for the backboard.

You also have a better idea than your opponent as to how a teammate's shot is spinning, so you should know how it will behave after it rebounds off the rim or backboard. This knowledge can help you to be in the right spot as the ball comes down.

When one of your teammate's shots misses and it rebounds close to the rim, you may be able to leap up and tap the ball toward the basket. Leap high, extending your arms and spreading your fingers.

Try to use both hands.

One tap probably won't do the job. You'll have to go up and tap again—and perhaps a third and fourth time. Each time you come down, be sure to land on the balls of your feet and sink in the knees, so you'll be able to spring back up.

If you leap up to tap and you're unable to get a clear shot at the basket, try tapping the ball back to one of your teammates. You'll have to arch it high so it will clear the defensive players.

Rebounding on free-throw attempts is more systemized. The rules designate where players are to position themselves. If your team has been awarded the foul, the opposition gets the inside positions on each side of the free-throw lane. A member of your team flanks each of these players.

When the ball goes up, the inside player takes her first step toward the foul line, attempting to box out the opposition player. One other rebounder from the defensive team is posted alongside the key not far from the shooter. Her job is to prevent the shooter from becoming a rebounder. As the shot is taken, she steps into the key in front of the shooter, blocking her path to the basket.

Being alert is the vital ingredient when you're attempting to rebound, and it doesn't matter whether the play involves a free throw or a field-goal attempt. It doesn't matter whether your team is attacking or playing defense. You should assume that every shot that goes up is going to miss—and be ready to grab it as it starts coming down.

TEAM DEFENSE

There are two styles of defensive basketball: player-to-player and zone. In a player-to-player defense, each member of a team is assigned to guard a particular opponent. In a zone defense, each guards a certain area of the court.

Some high schools stress the player-to-player style; others prefer the zone. Actually, they are not very different. Zone defense is simply the player-to-player style within certain defined areas. If you're skilled in player-to-player, then playing zone defense should be easy for you.

There are several advantages to the player-to-player style. Each member of the team knows in advance whom she is going to be covering, so there is never any conflict in this regard. You simply stay with your opponent wherever she moves, covering her on inbound plays, rebounds, when she sets up to shoot, when she drives, and even on free throws.

With the zone, there can be moments of confusion because the areas of coverage overlap. For

As one team surges upcourt, opposing players hurry to pick up their defensive assignments.

Full-court press begins as soon as opposition attempts a throw-in.

example, if you're a forward you may sometimes find your team's center or a guard edging into your zone when the ball is there.

Another advantage of using the player-to-player style is that it gives your coach control over the matchups. For instance, if the opposition has a player who is particularly tall, the coach can assign your team's tallest player to cover her. She can match speed against speed, power against power.

Still another reason why most coaches prefer player-to-player is because each player gets to know the opponent she's guarding. She gets to know which side of the court her opponent favors, her dribbling style, and her ability as a shotmaker. In zone play, since players cover several opponents, they're not likely to get to know the playing characteristics of any one of them.

Player-to-player defense can be adapted to the particular type of offense a team is facing or to a game situation. Players can be instructed to guard tight or loose; they can be assigned to pick up opposition players at half court or use a full-court press. This last-named strategy is used right after your team has scored. The opposition is attempting a throw-in. Immediately you and your teammates begin tight guarding, harassing the opposition players as they attempt to bring the ball upcourt. Your objective is to force a bad pass or some other mistake.

The full-court press is used in the late stages of a

game by a team that is trailing. It requires too much stamina to be attempted for an entire game.

Teams using a player-to-player defense sometimes sag, or collapse. When this happens, a defensive player drops off the opponent she's guarding to pick up another opponent who looms as a scoring threat. Occasionally two or three players may collapse on the opposition's pivot player.

One of the shortcomings of the player-to-player style can occur when the team includes a weak player, one who lacks in skill, stamina, or aggressiveness. The offense can create a mismatch involving the weak player, and thereby exploit her.

With the zone defense, on the other hand, it's possible to "hide" a weak player. The arrangement of zones can be adjusted so that the responsibilities of the weak player are assumed by her teammates.

As this suggests, there are several different types of zone defense. If a team has quick guards, what is called a 2-1-2 zone may be used. The most frequently used of the various zone formations, the 2-1-2 calls for one player to be stationed at about the free-throw line. The players are positioned near the backboard outside the free-throw lane. The remaining two players are positioned near the top of the

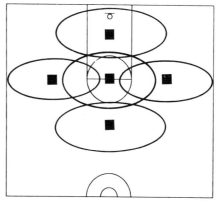

1-3-1 zone

key, to the right and left of the free-throw lane.

The 1-3-1 zone is used against a team that has a high-scoring center, probably a player who is much taller than average. But this formation is weak in the corners and on the outside, and good outside shooting can exploit these weaknesses.

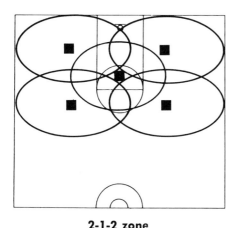

2-1-2 zone

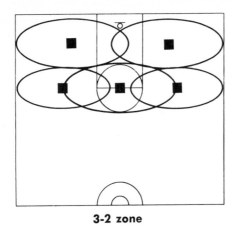

3-2 zone

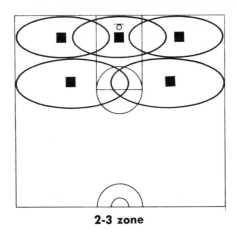

2-3 zone

The 3-2 zone is sometimes used against a team that is noted for its outside shooting skill. But it presents weaknesses near the baseline, because the two deep defenders must cover a very wide area of the court.

Finally, there is the 2-3 zone, which is employed against a team that shoots well from the baseline. It is vulnerable, however, to shots originating near the free-throw line.

As the opening paragraphs of this section stated, the techniques used in the player-to-player style and the zone are the same. The section that follows explains some of them.

DEFENSIVE PLAY

Forwards and centers used to think of themselves solely as offensive specialists, and worked to improve those skills best suited toward putting the ball in the basket. They expected their guards to prevent the opposition from scoring.

Not any more. In modern basketball, you can never be sure what's going to be happening. One second your team has the ball and is careening downcourt, but the next second something happens —there's a steal or an interception—and the opposition takes over, and you and your teammates are trying to prevent a field goal. Players today have to be just as skilled on defense as they are on offense.

There is a basic stance that players use on defense. The body is low, the knees slightly bent. The feet are at least shoulder-width apart.

One hand is held high, the arm fully extended, to block a shot or a pass and also to distract the player you're guarding. The other hand is extended out to the side, the arm about parallel to the floor. With this hand, you seek to block a pass or obstruct a dribble.

You move with a shuffle step. One foot moves to the side, the other follows, bringing you back to the basic stance position again. Say you're moving to your right. Your right foot moves first and then your left. As you continue to move, it's right-left, right-left, and so on. Keep the steps short, no more

On defense, move with a side-to-side shuffle step.

than six or seven inches in length.

Your feet must never cross when you're playing defense. Let this happen and you're sure to be off balance. You're then vulnerable to a quick move or feint.

"Hands up!" "Hands up!" coaches shout from the bench when they want their players to become tougher defensively. Some coaches have a hands-up drill they use in practice sessions. Players are sent out onto the court and instructed to take up positions about six feet apart. They then assume the basic defense stance described above, the feet apart, the knees flexed, one arm extended over the head, the other out to the side.

The coach then shouts out various commands: "Forward!" "Back!" "Right!" "Left!" The players take two or three shuffling steps in the direction called.

In practice sessions early in the season, the drill lasts about five minutes. Day by day, it's increased in length. At the University of California, the drill has lasted for as long as twenty minutes. By this time, many of the players are howling in pain.

Try this: Hold one arm straight out to the side and keep it in that position for four or five minutes. Notice how much pain develops in the muscles of the upper arm. Agonizing pain would result should you be made to hold the arms outstretched for many more minutes than five.

Coaches use the hands-up drill to teach the importance of keeping the hands in an upraised position. It's natural to want to drop the hands to your side. But do that when you're playing defense and the results are likely to be costly.

The drill also teaches players to be alert. If a player fails to move to the right when the coach calls out "Right!", she's likely to get bumped by the player on her left.

Hands-up posture is what prevents field goals.

Sometimes it's necessary to modify the basic hands-up position. When you're confronted by a player who is dribbling the ball, keep both arms parallel to the floor, one hand to the side, the other in front of you. Flick out with your front hand. But beware of "hacking," a word the rulebook defines as "hitting the wrist or forearm of an opponent" in an attempt to get the ball. Hacking is a personal foul.

When a game begins, one of the first things that you should do is diagnose the strengths and weaknesses of the player you're going to be guarding. Suppose she prefers dribbling and driving to her right. Once you've established that fact, make up your mind to overplay her on that side. Force her to go either farther to the right (which will take her a greater distance from the basket), or make her go to the left (the side on which she's weak and more vulnerable). This is basic defensive strategy.

Suppose the player that you're guarding gets past you, what then? Don't chase her. If you go after her, you'll simply trail her all the way to the basket and end up with an embarrassed look on your face as the ball swishes through the net.

Instead of pursuing an opponent who has driven past you, you must try to "beat her to the spot." This means that you must decide in the blink of an eye where she's going with the ball, and then get there before she does.

When the player you're covering stops dribbling

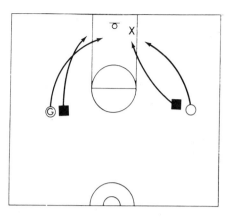

Guard (G) on left has driven past her defender, who pursues her to the basket. On the right, beaten defender turns to get to shooting area (X) before ball handler.

and gets set to shoot or pass, become even more aggressive. Move your hands; shout at her.

Do your best to deflect the ball away. Go for it from below, however. When you try to hit the ball from the top, you risk a hacking foul.

Watch out for a fake. Your opponent may suddenly thrust the ball upward as if she is going to execute a jump shot. But it's a feint. If you go for the fake and leap up to block the ball, she'll simply wait for you to go back down—and then shoot.

How do you avoid this? Never leave your feet until you see the opponent you're guarding leave hers.

How closely you play your opponent depends on

whether or not she has the ball. Naturally, she's more dangerous when she has the ball in her possession, so you must play her tighter than normal.

How tight you play an opponent also depends on your quickness—or lack of it. If you're quicker than normal, you don't have to play an opponent as close as the average player. You know that if your opponent should get by you, you can recover fast. But if a slow player gets beaten, an opposition basket is often the result.

Your height is a factor, too. If you are taller than the player you're guarding, you have a big advantage. You can play "off" your opponent somewhat. You don't have to harass her with your hands when she gets to shoot. You may be able to wait until the shot is in the air, and then block it.

If you're shorter than the player you're guarding, you have to be especially careful about guarding. Hustle; try to anticipate what your opponent is going to do. Be wary about trying to block the shot of an opponent who is taller than you are. There is a greater risk of fouling.

Keep alert for situations wherein you can assist a teammate on defense. Suppose an opponent with the ball is closer to the basket than the player you've been assigned to cover. This is an obvious time to help out a teammate. Turn toward the player who has the ball, ready to dart toward her should she seek to penetrate any closer.

Should the offensive player get free and drive for the basket, it may trigger a switch. Suppose the opposition player that you're guarding has set a screen for a teammate. The opposing player with the ball is free as a result. It's up to you to shout out "Switch!", and pick up the ball handler, making her change direction or pass. Your teammate moves to cover your player.

Once you've switched to another opponent, keep covering that opponent until there's a pause in play and you have a chance to switch back.

Switching serves as a good example of how on-the-court communication can help a team. You and your teammates should constantly be shouting out warnings and instructions to one another.

If your team suddenly gains control of the ball on a steal or intercepted pass, your coach may instruct you to shout out, "Ball! Ball!" Every player will then break downcourt. Should your team be the victim of a steal or an interception, "Back!" Back!" is what to yell. "Watch the backdoor!", "I need help!" or, simply, "Help! Help!" are shouts you hear from the floor.

THE RULES

In the years since Dr. Naismith first thought up the game of basketball, many different versions of the rules have been written. Elementary schools, high schools, colleges, and the professionals all play by different rules. But in each of the variations, certain fundamentals apply: The game is played by two teams of five players each, with each team trying to score points by shooting the ball into the opposition goal at the end of the court.

In girls' high school basketball, either one or two different sets of rules may be used. Most girls' teams —about three-quarters of them, in fact—are governed by rules set down by the National Federation of State High School Associations (Box 98, Elgin, Illinois 60120). They are known as the "Federation rules." A copy of the Federation rulebook can be ordered by mail. It costs $1.25.

Other girls' teams follow rules established by the National Association for Girls and Women in Sport (1201 Sixteenth Street, N.W., Washington, D.C. 20036). The NAGWS rulebook costs $1.50.

What makes the NAGWS rules different from the Federation rules is a pair of black boxes, each about the size of a breadbox, that are placed at opposing corners of the court, blinking out elapsed seconds from one to thirty. These are the 30-second shooting clocks, timing devices that have an important effect upon the game.

The 30-second clock

When a team gets possession of the ball following a throw-in, a jump ball, a rebound, or after any shot, the clocks start flashing in unison—1, 2, 3, 4, 5 . . . Should the team with the ball fail to get a shot away within the 30-second period, the team loses possession; that is, the other team takes over the ball. A loud horn blares whenever thirty seconds have ticked away. The 30-second clock is always used in women's college basketball.

With the 30-second rule, a team can't freeze the ball, can't attempt to retain possession of the ball for an extended period of time without any effort to score. Under the Federation rules, a team that is leading in the final minutes of a game will sometimes do this, letting the playing time expire. Or sometimes an obviously inferior team will attempt to freeze the ball throughout an entire game, hoping

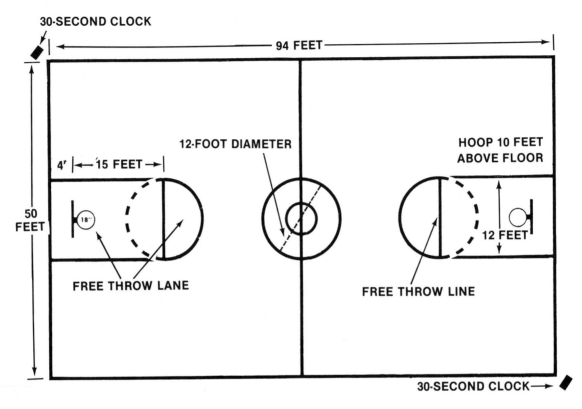

30-SECOND CLOCK

94 FEET

12-FOOT DIAMETER

HOOP 10 FEET ABOVE FLOOR

4' ← 15 FEET →|

50 FEET

18"

12 FEET

FREE THROW LANE

FREE THROW LINE

30-SECOND CLOCK →

to keep the score low and thereby increasing their chances of scoring an upset.

The 30-second clock prevents such tactics. Thirty seconds is the longest any team can stall.

The rectangular court for most high school games measures 94 feet (29 meters) by 50 feet (15 meters), but smaller courts are frequently used.

Most indoor courts are made of wood; however, composition surfaces are being used more and more. Outdoor courts are asphalt or concrete.

A sideline marks each side of the court. A baseline marks each end. A division line, a line parallel to the baselines, divides the court in half.

What is called a restraining circle marks the

center of the court. It has a diameter of 12 feet (3.7 meters).

A free-throw lane extends into the court from each baseline. In high school play, each lane is 12 feet (3.7 meters) in width and ends in a semicircle. A free-throw line, parallel to and 19 feet (5.8 meters) from the baseline, forms the diameter of each semicircle. A broken line inside the free-throw line completes the free-throw circle.

The backboards can be either of two types—rectangular or fan-shaped. Rectangular backboards are 72 inches (183 centimeters) wide and 48 inches (122 centimeters) high. Fan-shaped backboards are 54 inches (137 centimeters) wide and 35 inches (89 centimeters) high at their widest and highest

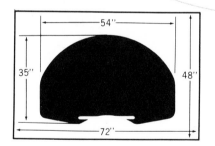

Backboard can be rectangular or fan-shaped.

points. Each backboard is mounted 4 feet (122 centimeters) inside the baseline.

The basket is a metal ring that is 18 inches (46 centimeters) in diameter, from which hangs a white cord net. The net is 15 to 18 inches (38 to 46 centimeters) long. The basket is mounted to the backboard near the bottom, with the plane of the ring parallel to the floor and 10 feet (3 meters) above it.

The ball weighs between 20 and 22 ounces (568 and 624 grams). It has a circumference of from 29½ to 30¼ inches (75 to 77 centimeters). When inflated to the specifications of the manufacturer and dropped to the playing court from a height of 6 feet (1.8 meters), it will bounce between 49 and 54 inches (1.2 meters and 1.3 meters).

Points are scored in two ways. A field goal, which counts 2 points, is scored by shooting the ball through the basket from anywhere on the court. Any player may score a field goal.

A free-throw shot, or foul shot, counts 1 point. A player who has been fouled may be awarded at least one free throw. She shoots the free throw from behind the free-throw line.

In high school play, a game lasts 32 minutes. It is divided into 16-minute halves, each of which is made up of 8-minute quarters. There is a 2-minute rest period between quarters, and a 10-minute rest period between halves. In the case of players younger than high school age, playing time may be less.

If the score is tied when time runs out, teams play as many overtime periods as are needed to reach a decision. High school teams play 3-minute overtimes, with a rest period of 2 minutes between each period.

During a game, time out is taken when an official calls a foul, when an official needs extra time to get the ball in play, on jump-ball plays, and when a team asks for a timeout.

In high school play, teams can call five timeouts during a game and one timeout in each overtime period. A timeout lasts 1 minute.

A basketball game starts with a jump ball. Any two opposing players face each other in the center restraining circle. The other players position themselves outside the circle. The referee tosses the ball into the air above the two players who jump up and try to tap the ball to one of their teammates.

Once a team gets the ball, the players begin working it toward the offensive basket. The players can advance the ball only by dribbling it, passing it to a teammate, or shooting it at the basket.

A team can lose possession of the ball for failing to handle it in a legal manner. Kicking the ball or striking it with the fists are other ball-handling violations. The ball is given over to the opposition out of bounds at the spot nearest to where the violation occurred.

The same penalty is assessed for traveling, double-dribbling, or causing the ball to go out of bounds. Traveling occurs when a player takes steps while in possession of the ball. A player double-dribbles

"Two shots!" signals the referee.

A tie ball—resulting in a jump.

when she bounces the ball with both hands at the same time or when she stops dribbling and then starts again. A ball is out of bounds when the ball itself or the player in possession of it touches or crosses a sideline or a baseline.

Ball-handling violations can also involve time restrictions. A team is not permitted to hold the ball for more than 5 seconds out of bounds. An offensive player is not permitted to stand in his team's free-throw lane for more than 3 seconds. This 3-second rule is meant to outlaw basket hanging, the practice of having a very tall player take up a position close to the basket, waiting for a pass which can easily be converted into an easy lay-up.

Under Federation rules, a team, after gaining control of the ball in its backcourt, must bring the ball into its forecourt within 10 seconds. When a team fails to do this, the other team is awarded the ball out of bounds.

Fouls, which are intended to prevent rough play and encourage freedom of movement, play a crucial role in every game. The most common type of foul is the personal foul. It occurs when a player pushes, holds, trips, or charges into an opponent who may or may not be in possession of the ball.

A player who is fouled in the act of shooting is awarded two free throws if she missed the field-goal attempt, and one free throw if she made it.

If the fouled player was not shooting, she may or may not be awarded one or more free throws. It depends on how many fouls have been committed by the opposition team during the half. In high school games, the fouled player is awarded an additional free throw if the opposition team has committed five or more personal fouls. If she makes that free throw, she gets another free-throw shot.

This additional free throw is a bonus shot. When a team fouls before the bonus situation is in effect, the ball is awarded to the opposition team out of bounds. This is also the penalty when a team in possession of the ball is guilty of a foul.

In each case, one foul is charged to the offending player. A player who commits five personal fouls is immediately disqualified from the game.

There are also technical fouls, which are called on a player or coach for unsportsmanlike conduct. A technical foul can be called on a player for using offensive language or addressing an official in a disrespectful manner. One can be called on a coach for substituting illegally, taking more than the legal number of timeouts, or leaving the bench to follow action on the court.

When a team is charged with a technical foul, the opposing team receives one free throw and then gets possession of the ball out of bounds at midcourt. Any player or coach who is guilty of three technical fouls is immediately disqualified from the game.

Close plays or disputed plays are sometimes settled by jump balls. For instance, when two opposing players touch the ball at the same time, causing it to go out of bounds, a jump ball is called.

A tie ball or a held ball also requires a jump ball. A tie ball occurs when two opposing players struggle for the ball without either gaining possession. A held ball is called when a closely guarded player holds the ball for more than five seconds. In each of these cases, the jump ball takes place in the center circle or in the free-throw circle nearest to the play.

A referee and an umpire supervise play. The referee is the official in charge, but the umpire has equal power in calling fouls and violations. One official usually takes up a position near the offensive team's basket, while the other official stays near the division line.

The referee and umpire are assisted by a scorer and timer. The scorer keeps a running score of the game and records all fouls. The timer is in charge of the game clock. There may also be an assistant timer, whose job it is to operate the 30-second clock.

GLOSSARY

AIAW—See Association for Intercollegiate Athletics for Women

ASSIST—A pass to a teammate which leads to a field goal.

ASSOCIATION FOR INTERCOLLEGIATE ATHLETICS FOR WOMEN—The governing body of women's college sports.

ATTEMPT—Any shot at the basket.

BACKBOARD—The rectangular or fan-shaped board from which the basket is suspended.

BACKCOURT—That half of the court that contains the basket a team is defending.

BASELINE—The line behind the basket that separates the court from the out-of-bounds area.

BASKET—The metal ring at each end of the court, 18 inches in diameter, from which hangs a white cord net, 15 to 18 inches in length.

BOARDS—The backboard.

BONUS SHOT—The additional free throw a team is awarded on all personal fouls after the opposing team has committed five personal fouls in a half.

BOXING OUT—Blocking out an opposition player by standing between her and the basket.

CENTER—The player who jumps at the center circle against an opposition player at the beginning of each quarter.

CENTER RESTRAINING CIRCLE—The circle, 12 feet in diameter, at midcourt.

COURT—The playing area; it cannot be bigger than 50 feet x 94 feet.

DEFENSIVE BASKET—The basket a team guards.

DEFENSIVE REBOUND—A rebound by a team near the basket it's defending.

DIVISION LINE—The court's center line.

DOUBLE-DRIBBLE—To bounce the ball with both hands at the same time or to stop dribbling and then start again.

DRIBBLE—To move the ball by means of repeated bounces.

FIELD GOAL—A basket from anywhere on the court. It counts 2 points.

FORECOURT—That half of the court containing the basket a team has under attack.

FORWARDS—The two players who, with the center, make up the front line of a team's offense. At the center jump, they line up nearest the offensive basket.

FOUL—An infraction of the rules for which one or more free throws may be awarded.

FOUL OUT—To be disqualified from play during a game for exceeding the number of permissible fouls. In high school competition, a player fouls out after five personal fouls or three technical fouls.

FOUL SHOT—See Free Throw.

FREE THROW—An unguarded throw to the basket from behind the free-throw line which is awarded a fouled player. A successful free throw counts 1 point.

FREE-THROW CIRCLE—The circular portion of the free-throw lane, 12 feet in diameter, which encloses the free-throw line.

FREE-THROW LANE—The 12-foot wide area in front of each basket that extends from the baseline to the free-throw line.

FREE-THROW LINE—A line 15 feet from the front plane of the backboard. Free throws are attempted from just behind the line.

FREEZE—To retain possession of the ball for an extended length of time without any attempt to score (in order to prevent one's opponent from gaining possession and scoring).

FULL-COURT PRESS—Tight guarding by a team, not only in its backcourt, but in its forecourt as well.

GUARDS—The two players who, at the center jump, line up farthest from the offensive basket.

HELD BALL—A game situation that occurs when a closely guarded player holds the ball for more than five seconds. A jump ball is the result.

JUMP BALL—A method of putting the ball in play in which an official tosses the ball into the air between opposing players, who try to tap it to teammates.

KEY; KEYHOLE—The entire free-throw area; it includes the free-throw lane and that portion of the free-throw circle beyond the free-throw line.

LANE—See Free-throw Lane.

LAY-UP—A one-handed banked shot made close to the basket.

LOB PASS—A soft, high, arcing pass.

NAGWS—See National Association for Girls and Women in Sport.

NATIONAL ASSOCIATION FOR GIRLS AND WOMEN IN SPORT—A national educational organization of teachers, coaches, and administrators, one of whose functions is to establish and interpret rules governing sports for girls and women.

NATIONAL FEDERATION OF STATE HIGH SCHOOL ASSOCIATIONS—A governing body of boys' and girls' high school sports.

OFFENSIVE BASKET—The basket a team has under attack.

OFFENSIVE REBOUND—A rebound by the

team on the attack near the basket it's attacking.

OUTLET PASS—A pass used to trigger a team's fast break following a rebound or a steal.

OUTSIDE SHOT—Any shot attempted over a long distance.

PERSONAL FOUL—An infraction of the rules that involves contact with an opposing player.

PICK—A screen play in which the player with the ball drives to the basket and shoots.

PLAYER-TO-PLAYER—A type of defense in which each member of the defensive team is assigned to cover a particular member of the team on offense.

PRESS; PRESSING—Tight guarding by the defensive team.

REBOUND—A missed shot that strikes the backboard or rim.

REFEREE—The official in charge of the game.

RESTRAINING CIRCLE—See Center Restraining Circle.

SAGGING—A type of defense in which a player drops off the girl she is guarding to cover a player nearer the basket.

SCORER—The official who keeps a running score of the game and records all fouls.

SCREEN—A maneuver by an offensive player in which she positions herself so as to block an opponent's path to a teammate with the ball.

SWITCH—A maneuver in which one defensive player exchanges responsibilities with a teammate.

TAP; TAP-IN—A lightly tipped shot off a rebound.

TECHNICAL FOUL—An infraction of the rules by a player or coach that involves unsportsmanlike conduct.

30-SECOND CLOCK—The timing device used to indicate the time remaining before a team in possession of the ball must try for a goal.

THROW-IN—The method of putting the ball in play from out of bounds.

TIE BALL—A game situation that occurs when two opposing players struggle for the ball without either being able to gain possession. A jump ball is the result.

TIMEOUT—The 60-second interval during which play is halted and the clock stopped.

TIMER—The official in charge of the game clock.

TRAVELING—Taking steps while in possession of the ball.

UMPIRE—The game official who is second in command to the referee, but with powers equal to the referee's in calling fouls and violations.

VIOLATION—Breaking a rule that results in a team losing possession of the ball or in a jump ball.

ZONE DEFENSE—A type of defense in which each member of the defensive team covers a particular area of the court.